Chemtastrophe!

Environmental Chemistry

Rachel Eagen

Crabtree Publishing Company
www.crabtreebooks.com

Crabtree Publishing Company
www.crabtreebooks.com

Publishing plan research and development:

Sean Charlebois, Reagan Miller
Crabtree Publishing Company

Developed and Produced by: Plan B Book Packagers

Editorial director: Ellen Rodger

Art director: Rosie Gowsell-Pattison

Glossary and index: David Pula

Project coordinator: Kathy Middleton

Editor: Adrianna Morganelli

Proofreader: Crystal Sikkens

Prepress technician and production coordinator:

Margaret Amy Salter

Print coordinator: Katherine Berti

Special thanks to experimenters Nico and Natasha

Photographs: Title page: Lisa F. Young/Shutterstock Inc.; p.2 : Johann Kerseboom/Wikimedia Commons; p. 3: Teacept/Shutterstock Inc.; p. 4: Supri Suharjoto/Shutterstock Inc.; p. 5: Huguette Roe/Shutterstock Inc.; p. 6: Vaclav Volrab/Shutterstock Inc.; p. 7: Tropic Dreams/Shutterstock Inc.; p. 8: Joe White/Shutterstock Inc.; p. 9: (top) Konovalikov Andrey/Shutterstock Inc., (bottom) Don Bendickson/Shutterstock Inc.; p. 10: A. Längauer/Shutterstock Inc.; p. 11: Antonio Abrignani/Shutterstock Inc.; p. 12: Elena Stepanova/Shutterstock Inc.; p. 13: (top) Greenland/Shutterstock Inc., (bottom) Johann Kerseboom/Wikimedia Commons; p. 14: Robert Fullerton/Shutterstock Inc.; p. 15: Jose Gil/Shutterstock Inc.; p. 16: Barnaby Chambers/Shutterstock Inc.; p. 17: (top) Walter G Arce/Shutterstock Inc., (bottom) Johann Kerseboom/Wikimedia Commons; p. 18: Monkey Business Images/Shutterstock Inc.; p. 19: Laurence Gough/Shutterstock Inc.; p. 20-23: Jim Chernishenko; p. 24: sbmverbi/Shutterstock Inc.; p. 25: (top) PeJo/Shutterstock Inc., (bottom) Johann Kerseboom/Wikimedia Commons; p. 26: (bottom) Sebastian Kaulitzki/Shutterstock Inc., (top) Sashkin /Shutterstock Inc.; p. 27: (top) Denisk/Shutterstock Inc., (bottom) Khram/Shutterstock Inc.; p. 28: Reflekta/Shutterstock Inc.; p. 29: Nomad Soul/Shutterstock Inc.; p. 30-31: Teacept/Shutterstock Inc.

"How we know" boxes feature an image of 17th century Irish chemist, physicist, and inventor Robert Boyle who is best remembered for his experiments with the volume and pressure of gases. The results from his experiments became known as Boyle's Law.

Library and Archives Canada Cataloguing in Publication

Eagen, Rachel, 1979-
    Environmental chemistry / Rachel Eagen.

(Chemtastrophe!)
Includes index.
Issued also in electronic format.
ISBN 978-0-7787-5285-1 (bound).--ISBN 978-0-7787-5302-5 (pbk.)

    1. Environmental chemistry--Juvenile literature.
2. Pollution--Juvenile literature. 3. Chemistry--Experiments--Juvenile literature. I. Title. II. Series: Chemtastrophe!

TD193.E23 2011   j628.501'54   C2010-906576-X

Library of Congress Cataloging-in-Publication Data

Eagen, Rachel, 1979-
 Environmental chemistry / Rachel Eagen.
    p. cm. -- (Chemtastrophe!)
Includes index.
 ISBN 978-0-7787-5302-5 (pbk. : alk. paper) -- ISBN 978-0-7787-5285-1
(reinforced library binding : alk. paper) -- ISBN 978-1-4271-9610-1
(electronic (pdf))
 1. Environmental chemistry--Juvenile literature. 2. Pollution--Juvenile literature. I. Title.
TD193.E15 2011
628.501'54--dc22

                    2010042063

Crabtree Publishing Company

www.crabtreebooks.com   1-800-387-7650

Printed in China/012011/GW20101014

Published in Canada
Crabtree Publishing
616 Welland Ave.
St. Catharines, ON
L2M 5V6

Published in the United States
Crabtree Publishing
PMB 59051
350 Fifth Avenue, 59th Floor
New York, New York 10118

Published in the United Kingdom
Crabtree Publishing
Maritime House
Basin Road North, Hove
BN41 1WR

Published in Australia
Crabtree Publishing
386 Mt. Alexander Rd.
Ascot Vale (Melbourne)
VIC 3032

Contents

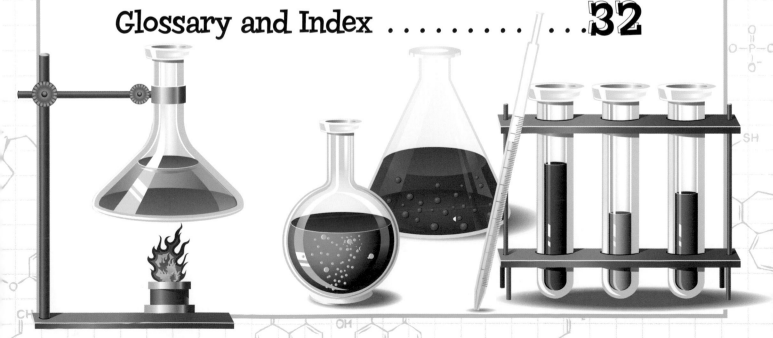

Science and Discovery

What do you think of when you hear the word chemistry? Most people think of a scientist in a white lab coat, conducting experiments. You might not realize that chemistry is everywhere. Chemical processes control how much rain and snow fall to the earth, as well as how long it takes for garbage to break down in landfills.

What is Science?

Science is the study of the physical and natural world. Science is all about observation and experimentation—looking at the world, asking questions, and trying to find answers to those questions. Scientists are people who research and study science. They gather information in a systematic way, develop **theories**, and perform experiments that involve testing ideas. Science is a huge field, and chemistry is just one branch of many different kinds of science. Chemistry involves looking at the way living and nonliving things react with **substances** in the environment.

Scientists work just about everywhere: in laboratories, in educational institutions, out in "the field," and in industry.

fun fact

Photosynthesis is the name given to a chemical process that plants use to feed themselves. With the help of sunlight, water, and a gas in the atmosphere called carbon dioxide, plants create a sugary food that helps them grow.

4

Early Science

It is in our nature to be curious about our world. The very first humans wanted to know more about their surroundings, which led them to try new things and make discoveries. You can think of discoveries as lucky accidents, because it is just about impossible to know what will happen when you try something for the first time. One of the first accidental discoveries happened when humans learned how to make and use fire. They used it to cook food, and to harden clay into vessels. Learning to use fire was an important development in chemistry, because it led to so many other discoveries.

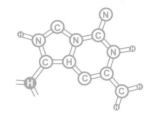

Chemistry

Chemistry is the study of matter. Matter is everything you can see, as well as everything you cannot see. The study of chemistry is also about creating and observing chemical reactions, in which two or more things react, or work together, to create something new. Chemists study the properties, or nature of things, in the world around us, as well as substances that are created in labs. They watch carefully to see how chemicals behave and how matter changes under different circumstances.

Many different chemical processes, such as the water and nitrogen cycles, happen naturally. These processes not only give us weather and break down garbage, they also help pollutants to enter our water, air, and land.

About Matter

Matter is, plain and simple, everything. The entire world is made up of matter, including trees, animals, buildings, and even you. Understanding the way matter behaves is an important part of chemistry.

Atoms and Molecules

Matter is made up of **particles** that are so tiny that you cannot see them without the help of a powerful microscope. These particles hold onto each other, forming a blob of material that you can see on your own, such as a leaf, a grain of sand, or a drop of water. These particles are called atoms. Atoms have three parts: protons, neutrons, and electrons. The protons and neutrons bind together in the center of the atom, forming the nucleus. The electrons orbit, or spin, around the nucleus in ring patterns. It is impossible to see these rings because the electrons move so quickly, which is why scientists describe the movement of electrons as an electron cloud. Each part of an atom carries a tiny charge. Protons carry a positive charge, while the electrons carry a negative charge. The neutrons carry a neutral charge—neither positive nor negative. When two or more atoms cling together, it is called a molecule.

Yep, that drop of dew, blade of grass, and ladybug, are all matter.

Solid

Matter can be in one of three states: solid, liquid, or gas. In each of these states, the atoms that make up matter move, but the movement is impossible to see. For example, when you look at a single fingernail, you cannot tell that there are millions of atoms vibrating within it. Atoms and molecules move differently depending on the state of matter they are in. In a solid, the atoms move very little. They are packed together very tightly, allowing the solid to keep its shape.

Liquid

In a liquid, atoms are spaced further apart. They are attracted to each other, but they have more space between them to move more freely. That is why liquids can flow, or be poured. Liquids can move quickly, as in a stream, or slowly, as in a pond. All liquids take the shape of the container that holds them, such as the concrete walls of a pool, or the muddy bottom of a riverbed.

And Gas

The atoms of a gas are spaced furthest apart. Gases take up as much as they possibly can, eventually spreading out so thin that you might not see them at all. Just think of the thick black smoke that blows out from the chimneys of a factory. The smoke rises into the sky and spreads out, eventually seeming to disappear.

Vapor rises from a smokestack, spreading out as a gaseous form of matter.

Clouds are water vapor.

The Water Cycle

States of matter do not have to stay the same. Matter can change states as it gains or loses energy. One way to give matter energy is to heat it up. This is exactly what happens on the surface of oceans, lakes, and other bodies of water every day. As the sun shines on the surface of water, the water heats up. In other words, the water molecules at the surface of the water start to move more quickly and spread out, eventually gaining so much energy that they rise into the air as water vapor. This is known as evaporation. In this gaseous state, the water molecules start to cool off when they are in the air. The water molecules lose energy as they cool down, eventually losing so much energy that they pull closer together to become a liquid again. This process, condensation, is what forms clouds. Over time, so much water gathers that the clouds become very heavy, and the water comes back to the earth as precipitation—rain, snow, or hail.

fun fact

Each year, the United States consumes over seven billion barrels of oil, close to one-quarter of the total world consumption.

Elements and Compounds

Atoms are not all the same. In fact, scientists have identified over 100 different kinds of atoms. They differ depending on how many protons they have in their nucleus. Every different kind of atom is called an element, and all of the known atoms belong to a chart known as the periodic table of elements. This table is very important to chemists around the world. In the table, the elements are listed according to how many protons they have. For example, the first element is called hydrogen. It has a single proton, and for this reason, it has the atomic number 1. When two or more different kinds of atoms, or elements combine, they create a new substance called a compound molecule, which chemists simply call compounds. A water molecule, for example, is a compound made up of two hydrogen atoms and one oxygen atom.

In chemistry terms, water is a compound of two atoms.

Alchemists believed that matter, such as copper or nickel, could be transformed into gold.

The Birth of Chemistry

Chemistry has been around from the beginning of time, long before there was life on Earth. However, chemistry was not always considered a real science. In 1661, British scientist Robert Boyle published *The Sceptical Chymist*, a book in which he explained why chemistry was a true scientific field of study, different from other fields. Until this point, chemistry was more closely associated with alchemy. Alchemists were known for their attempts to create gold from common metals. In *The Sceptical Chymist*, Boyle outlined some important ideas about atoms, molecules, and chemical reactions. Many believe this work marks the beginning of modern chemistry.

The Method of Science

Scientific discoveries are often made when scientists are least expecting it. That is not because they do not know what they are doing. Just about anything can happen during an experiment, and good scientists are always ready to have their ideas proven right or wrong—because either way, these discoveries lead to a better understanding of our world.

Ancient Scientists

Thousands of years ago, the field of science was rooted in a tradition known as philosophy. Back then, philosophers thought about human existence and the meaning of life, as well as other ideas about nature. The ancient philosophers believed that there were four basic elements that were the building blocks of all life. They were: water, earth, fire, and air. Today, scientists think of elements a lot differently. However, the ancient philosophers were onto something, as they made predictions. A prediction is sort of like a guess, although modern scientists usually make what they call educated guesses. That means that their guesses are based on things they already know to be true.

Ancient philosophers made observations based on what they knew of the world.

fun fact

The word "element" first appeared in 360 BC, in a collection of writings by the ancient philosopher Plato.

Testing

Today, scientists have to prove their ideas and educated guesses with research. The best way to conduct research is to try out an idea in real life, by experimentation. In an experiment, a scientist **simulates** an event under controlled conditions. In other words, the scientist makes sure that the experiment happens in conditions that do not change, such as in a lab, using the same tools, making accurate and **consistent** measurements. Controlled conditions are important for producing similar results experiment after experiment. Scientists usually have to prove their findings several times, which means doing the experiment over and over again—sometimes hundreds of times!

Models, Theories, Laws

After a lot of experimentation, scientists try to describe their findings by creating a model. Models are usually physical representations or mathematical **equations**. For example, Danish **physicist** Niels Bohr (1885-1962), who is known for his ideas about atoms, developed several models to explain why atoms behave the way they do. These models were oversized versions of the atoms we cannot see. Models are very important for scientists to explain their work in a way that can be easily understood by other scientists. Once scientists have tested an idea several times, they put together theories that explain their findings. Theories explain things that recur in nature. They are based on large, detailed bodies of research and can represent many years of research. These theories may be shortened into scientific laws, which are simple statements of scientific truths.

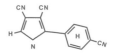

Niels Bohr developed the atomic theory.

Everyday Chemistry

From the foods we eat, the products we buy in stores, and the clothing we wear, chemistry is a big part of our everyday lives. It is impossible to get through a single day without bumping into chemistry in some way.

A Dip in the Pool

Imagine waking up on a hot summer day. What sorts of things would you like to do? You might stay cool by going for a swim in a local pool. Did you know that this would be impossible without chemistry? Many swimming pools use strong chemicals, such as chlorine or bromine, to kill harmful bacteria. Chlorine and bromine also help get rid of **contaminants** that affect the pH of the pool, such as sweat, saliva, bird droppings, and sunscreen. The pH scale is used to determine how acidic or basic a substance is. The scale goes from 0 to 14. Substances that have a pH of 6 or less are said to be acidic, while substances with a pH of 8 or more are described as basic. A pH of 7 is said to be neutral. Both acidic and basic products can be very harmful if they come in contact with the human body. That is why it is very important that pool water maintains a pH of 7.2 to 7.8, which is more or less neutral.

If the water were any more basic, the chlorine would lose some effectiveness and not clean the water properly. Acidic pool water would make swimmers' skin itch and burn.

There are about 95,000 chemists working in the United States today.

Chemistry in Other Places

What else would you like to do on a hot, sunny day? How about sitting under a tree with a good book? Books are also products of chemistry. Special chemicals are used to process trees into sheets of paper, which is then bleached white. Chemical inks are used to print words on the pages, and still more chemicals are used in the glue that binds the pages together. How about a cool drink for your afternoon in the shade? A cool drink of lemonade is the result of chemical processes in the food industry. Chemical sweeteners are used in drinks made from concentrate, and still more chemicals are used to make plastic, metal, or cardboard packaging that is used to hold frozen juices. Even the glass you use to drink from is a product of chemistry, as glass and plastic must be treated in special ways to make it safe for human use.

Chemistry is even involved in making books!

HOW WE KNOW

Preventing Chemtastrophes

One of the main functions of everyday chemistry is safety. Chemists around the world are constantly testing the products we buy, eat, and use on our bodies to make sure that they are safe. Chemists work in water filtration plants, where water from large bodies of water is treated to make it suitable for drinking. Chemists also monitor the safety of chemicals that are used by farmers, not only for our own health, but also for the health of our planet and the animals in it.

Enviro Chemistry

Earth's water, air, and land are polluted by millions of different chemicals. Major industries are often to blame, but on a smaller scale, we contribute to polluting Earth on a daily basis. Knowing the chemistry of these pollutants and how they hurt the planet is important for finding ways to clean them up.

Acid rain

Acid rain is a term for rain, snow, hail, fog, and any other kind of precipitation that has a lower pH than regular rainwater. A pH below 7 is described as acidic, and just as acids can hurt your skin, acid rain can hurt the planet. So, how is acid rain made? It starts with toxic **emissions** that are pumped into the air from the chimneys of large factories, cars, and our own homes. Two of the biggest culprits of acid rain are chemicals called sulphur dioxide and nitrogen oxide. These poisons mix invisibly in the air, eventually working their way into clouds and falling to the earth as precipitation. Over time, acid rain erodes hard surfaces such as marble, granite, brick, and metal. Acid rain also runs into lakes and rivers. Acid rain can be a chemtastrophe for fish and wildlife by "killing" lakes. Acid rain also affects trees, which lose their leaves or needles, or turn a yellow or rust color. Acid damage can also be seen on the bark of trees. In parts of the world where there is heavy coal-burning industry, such as China, entire forests have been lost to acid rain.

Pollution causes the chemtastrophe known as acid rain.

Ozone Good and Bad

One of the biggest environmental problems today is the air we breathe. Living things need to breathe oxygen to stay alive. When the air is polluted with toxic chemicals, we are put at risk for health problems, such as **asthma** and other lung disorders. Ozone is a molecule made up of three oxygen atoms. There are two kinds of ozone: stratospheric ozone and ground-level ozone. Ozone shields the surface of Earth from harmful ultraviolet rays in Earth's atmosphere. Atmospheric, or stratospheric ozone is known as "good ozone." Closer to the ground, ozone is formed from air pollution that is created by burning fossil fuels. Pollutants, including nitrogen oxide gases, combine with oxygen and heat from the Sun to form ozone. Since sunlight helps produce ozone, higher levels of ozone are produced on very hot days. High concentrations of ozone help create dirty air known as smog. This smog breaks down living tissue in our lungs, making it harder to breathe. That is why people are advised to stay indoors when there is a smog alert. The silver lining is that ozone breaks down once conditions cool down.

Smog is a chemical soup that makes it difficult to breathe.

15

fun fact

"The more clearly we can focus our attention on the wonders and realities of the universe about us, the less taste we shall have for destruction."
–Rachel Carson, environmentalist

Persistent Organic Pollutants

Ozone is not the only toxin responsible for polluting our air. Persistent Organic Pollutants (POPs) are other byproducts of industry and the burning of fossil fuels. These pollutants take a long time to break down. Some of the most well known POPs are chemicals called polychlorinated biphenyls (PCBs), which come from **coal tar**, and were once used in waxes, lubricants, and inks. Dioxins are chemicals that are made from the burning of waste and fossil fuels, and in the production of fungicides and herbicides. The pesticide DDT is another well-known POP. Many countries, including the United States, have realized the harm of POPs and have created laws to ensure that they are not produced anymore.

Petrochemicals are used in the pharmaceutical industry, as it is the basis of many important medicines such as ibuprofen and other painkillers.

Chemistry and Fossil Fuels

A huge portion of the energy we use every day is produced through the burning of fossil fuels. There are three types of fossil fuels: petroleum, coal, and natural gas. Petroleum has many uses, but one of its main applications is in the making of gasoline and diesel to power cars and trucks. Petroleum is also used to make **synthetic** materials, such as plastic, as well as paints. Coal is burned at power plants to generate electricity, and natural gas is often burned to heat homes and cook food. Fossil fuels concern environmentalists because they harm the environment through their extraction, chemical processing, and use.

When Chemistry Kills

In 1939, a Swiss chemist invented a chemical called dichlorodiphenyltrichloroethane (DDT). It was given to soldiers to sprinkle on their lice-infested clothing. Farmers also sprayed DDT on their fields to rid crops of pests. DDT became the most widely used pesticide for large-scale agriculture. DDT had a downside: birds began dropping dead, and they laid eggs with shells so thin that the birds died before they could hatch. Scientist Rachel Carson researched why this was happening. She realized that the chemical was also creeping into human food supply through **residues** that remained on grains, fruits, and vegetables that had been sprayed with DDT. Carson's most frightening realization was that once DDT entered the body, it stayed there forever, causing long-term health problems. The U.S. government responded to Carson's research by banning the use of DDT in 1972.

HOW WE KNOW

Bhopal Gas Chemtastrophe

If we aren't careful, chemistry can create horrible disasters, including the world's worst industrial catastrophe. In 1984, at the Union Carbide pesticide plant in Bhopal, India, a leak of toxic gases threatened over 500,000 people. Nearly 4,000 people died within the first day of exposure, but many more died of related illnesses in the weeks and years that followed, eventually killing about 15,000 and leaving others maimed or in poor health. Thousands of animals were also killed. Trees in the area dropped all of their leaves within a few days of the accident. Toxic chemicals continue to leak into the groundwater at the site of the leak, poisoning the water supply of the people who live in Bhopal.

Testing Theories

A big part of being a chemist is conducting experiments to test your ideas. All scientific experimentation involves thinking about good questions, researching the best possible way to find an answer to those questions, and gathering information that might explain the results of the experiment.

Following Steps

Scientists follow six basic steps when they experiment: stating a purpose, researching, making a hypothesis, conducting an experiment, making observations, and explaining the results to reach a conclusion. Step 1 is usually stating your purpose as a question. What do you want to know? This question can be simple or complicated, but it should be stated as a single question or statement.

Research can be done at a library or anywhere information can be accessed.

Research

This is when you gather as much information as you can about the question you are trying to answer. Research helps you prepare for the experiment. What kinds of tools will you need to conduct your experiment? Sometimes, research gives you a better idea of how the experiment might turn out, especially if you are modifying an experiment that someone else has already done.

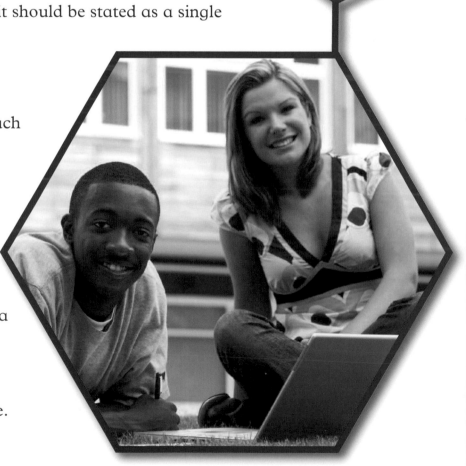

18

Make a Hypothesis

A hypothesis is an educated guess, or prediction, about what will happen during the experiment. A hypothesis is a statement that goes something like: If I…this will happen.

The Experiment

This is where you explain what you are going to do. You may also choose to list all of the tools you will be using in the experiment, such as a beaker, measuring cup, and other items. Break the experiment down into small steps that are easy to follow. Remember to include a timeframe for the steps that require extra time. For example, waiting for a seed to sprout may take seven days or more, and you should note that in your experiment.

Observations and Conclusions

This is where you explain everything that you observe, or see, during the experiment. It helps to take notes during the experiment so you will not forget to include anything in your write-up later. Sometimes, this is called analysis. What happened? Were you surprised? Was your hypothesis correct? In this section, you explain what you discovered during the experiment. It is okay if your hypothesis was "wrong," just be sure to record your results honestly. Remember, experimentation is all about learning and having fun.

Sharing your observations adds to the scientific body of knowledge.

Polymer Slimeball

Have you ever wondered what makes some things stretchy and what makes others rigid?

Question: Can you make something out of a liquid and a solid that has qualities of both?

Hypothesis: Slime is a hybrid of liquid and solid, but is different from both.

Materials:

- 1/2 cup (118 ml) of water
- 1/2 tablespoon (7 grams) Borax powder (found in hardware or grocery stores)
- 3 to 6 tablespoons (45 to 90 ml) white craft glue
- 2 bowls
- spoons

Method:

1. Mix the Borax powder and 1/2 cup of water in one bowl.
2. Mix the glue and 2 or 3 spoonfuls of water in the other bowl.
3. Add a tablespoon of the Borax solution to the glue solution. Add more as needed.

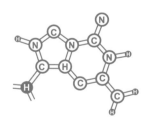

Measure and mix the Borax with water.

Measure the glue and mix with a couple spoonfuls of water in another bowl. Add a spoonful of the Borax mixture to the glue mixture.

Observe and record what happens.

Results and Discussion:

When the Borax mixture was mixed with the glue and water, it formed a lumpy blob of slime.

This slime is a polymer, or polyvinyl acetate. It has the qualities of a solid and a liquid. Polymer molecules bend and stretch and chain themselves together. Polymers are everywhere: in nylon clothing, plastic soda bottles, and most types of plastics.

What happens when you add more Borax solution, or less?

Enviro Cleaner

In this experiment, you will learn how easy it is to substitute non-toxic substances for cleaners that are harsh on the environment.

Question: Can cleaning products be made from everyday household materials?

Hypothesis: An environmentally friendly chemical reaction can clean silver just as well as harsh chemicals.

Materials:

aluminum foil
boiling water
baking soda
salt
tarnished silver plates
   or jewelry
spoon

Procedure:

1. Line a basin or sink with foil
2. Fill the bottom with baking soda and a bit of salt
3. Pour boiling water into basin.
4. Drop in the tarnished silver and wait.

Line a basin with aluminum foil and add baking soda and salt. Pour in boiling water and stir.

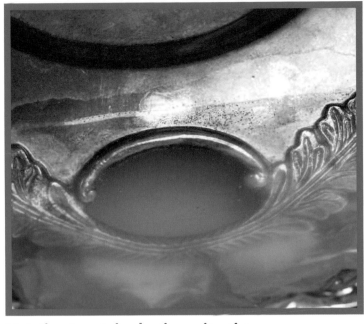

Put the tarnished silver (in this case a silver-plated platter) into the basin.

Wait 15 minutes, then observe and record.

Results and Discussion:

As silver oxidizes, or is exposed to air, it tarnishes, or turns a black color. This layer of oxidization can be removed without harming the environment by causing a minor chemical reaction. In this experiment, the silver that touches the aluminum undergoes a chemical reaction.

Does the tarnish come off of the parts of the silver that did not touch the aluminum? Why not?

Eureka!

There have been some great discoveries in chemistry that have changed our lives. Some have made life less difficult, but many have led to environmental destruction.

Lighting the Way

Kerosene is a thin, clear fluid that has many practical uses. It is made through the **distillation** of crude oil. The first record of kerosene is in writings by Razi, a Persian scholar who produced it by using an alembic, which is an apparatus made of two glass containers connected by a single tube. Razi may have created kerosene by accident, but many who came after him adopted his technique to perfect the distillation process. Kerosene is an amazing discovery because it has so many different uses. It can power engines and rockets. It is used as fuel in oil lamps and camping stoves. Kerosene was once used in most chemical **pesticides**, and can be used to kill bed bugs, lice, and mosquitoes. Kerosene is excellent for removing glue and other adhesives, and may also be used as a lubricant to cut glass.

Kerosene is highly flammable, which makes it useful to fire breathers.

Changing Stockings

Nylon was invented in 1935 by Wallace Carothers at a DuPont research lab in Wilmington, Delaware. Nylon is a synthetic material, meaning it does not occur in nature by itself. It is made by combining smaller atoms or molecules to create large chains, or polymers. Nylon was a very important discovery, as it is now one of the most widely used polymers in industry today. It was first used in 1938 to make toothbrush bristles, but nylon became more widely known when it was used to create women's stockings. Today, it is widely used in clothing, as well as in mechanical parts, such as nylon screws and gears. It is very durable and can be molded.

The invention of nylon has made many things possible.

HOW WE KNOW

The Chemistry of Plastics

Plastics are polymers that are used to make millions of different products, including soft drink bottles, material for clothing, electric fans, car parts, dishes, pipes, and hundreds of other products you use every day. In 1855, British inventor Alexander Parkes made plastic while trying to create synthetic ivory. He made the material by treating cellulose, a material found in plants, with nitric acid. His discovery, which he named Parkesine, won the bronze medal at the World's Fair in London, in 1862. Plastics are a huge part of our world today, but plastics have one major downfall: they take a very long time to break down in the environment. That means that plastics in our landfills may be there for years.

Creative Chemists

Chemistry is a science of new discovery. The process of discovery is almost always the same: scientists work in their labs in search of answers through experimentation. The results are sometimes surprising, but many of these surprises have changed the way we live.

Atomic Theory

Greek philosopher Democritus (c. 460-370 BC) was the first person to suggest that matter is made up of tiny particles that we cannot see. He named these particles atoms. This was the beginning of what chemists call atomic theory. In 1800, British scientist John Dalton contributed some new ideas about atoms. Dalton noted the following:

1) All elements are made up of atoms, and the atoms of one element are different from the atoms of other elements.
2) All atoms of the same element are identical.
3) Elements can combine to form compounds, which he called molecules.
4) Atoms (matter) cannot be created or destroyed. A chemical reaction changes the way atoms or molecules are arranged. Dalton's atomic theory **revolutionized** chemistry, because it helped other scientists to better understand the way atoms behave. It also gave scientists a better idea of what happens during a chemical reaction.

The Nobel Prize in Chemistry is the most prestigious award that a chemist can earn. The first one was awarded in 1901.

Modern Chemistry

Antoine Lavoisier was a French **nobleman** born in 1743. He is thought of as the "father of modern chemistry," as he contributed many ideas that remain important in the field of chemistry today. In the early 1700s, scientists explained combustion (burning) with the phlogiston theory. The main idea behind this theory was that all matter was infused with a weightless substance call phlogiston, and materials that had a lot of phlogiston burned easily. Lavoisier proved this theory wrong by explaining that combustion had nothing to do with phlogiston, but with oxygen. He went on to develop other laws of chemistry.

Antoine Lavoisier

Eugene Houdry

French engineer Eugene Houdry is credited with changing the petrochemical industry in the early 1930s, by inventing a chemistry process called catalytic cracking. Crude oil had been refined commercially since 1859, meaning it was processed on a large scale to produce gasoline to fuel some of the first cars. By the early 1900s, a gasoline shortage made scientists want to learn how to produce gasoline more efficiently. Houdry began experimenting with a type of coal called lignite. He found that he could speed up the process of converting oil from lignite to gasoline by using a catalyst. A catalyst is something that speeds up a chemical reaction, and the one Houdry used was called Fuller's Earth, a mineral that comes from clay. It is because of Houdry's invention, catalytic cracking, that goods can be shipped far distances from where they are made or grown. In fact, catalytic cracking is used to produce more than half of the gasoline that is used each day in the United States. Houdry's invention also led to the creation of thousands of jobs in the petrochemical industry.

Petroleum, or crude oil, is made of chains of hydrocarbons, or molecules made of hydrogen and carbon atoms.

Chemistry Today

It is hard to believe that just a few hundred years ago, chemistry was not even recognized as a real science. Today, there are dozens of different areas of chemistry.

Everything is Chemistry

There are many fields of study in chemistry. Chemists work in industry and manufacturing, education, and even government. Biochemistry is the study of chemicals and chemical reactions in living organisms (humans, plants, and animals). Neurochemistry is the study of brain chemicals that control the way people feel and behave. Other areas of chemistry overlap with different fields of study, such as chemical engineering, which includes the development of fuel, explosives, and other forms of technology. As the environment becomes a widespread concern, some chemists specialize in an area of study called environmental impact assessment. This type of study analyzes the possible effects of new technology on our environment. Chemists who work in this field of study may advise governments on the harmful practices of large corporations and the general public so that laws can be created to protect the environment.

Chemists love to experiment! It is one area where they can prove their theories.

What Do Chemists Do?

Some chemists work in labs where they try to develop new products and technologies. Some test environmental samples of water, air, and soil for toxicity, and look for ways to reduce pollution. Some chemists work to develop chemical weapons. Other types of chemists do not create products, and they do not spend any time in labs. Some analyze information for big companies, while others work in government, making sure that the right policies are in place to protect us as well as the environment. There are also many jobs for chemists who teach in high schools, colleges, and universities.

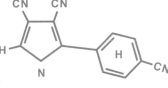

Becoming a Chemist

It takes work and dedication to become a chemist. Most chemists have a bachelor's degree from a university, but many go on to pursue PhDs. If you think you want to become a chemist, it is a good idea to study as much science and math as you can in high school. In some countries, chemists have to register themselves as professional chemists. Registering proves a person has completed all of the required education and experience to work in chemistry.

Chemists work in education and in industry.

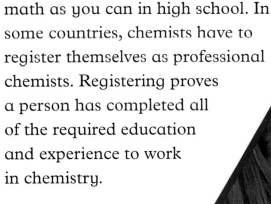

Want to Learn More?

The world of chemistry is exciting and ever changing. If you want to learn more about the chemistry of everyday life, check out some of the fascinating resources listed here.

Chemistry Websites:

Rader's Chem4Kids!
www.chem4kids.com/index.html
A fascinating website that offers an introduction to things like atoms, molecules, reactions, and much more. Games and quizzes are also available on the site.

BrainPop
www.brainpop.com/science/matterandchemistry/
Find answers to all your chemistry questions! This interactive site makes learning fun with the help of games, videos, and fascinating animations.

Science Made Simple
www.sciencemadesimple.com/
Get some great ideas for your next science project, and find fun chemistry activities you can do at home or with your friends and family.

Extreme Science
www.extremescience.com/zoom/index.php
Learn the science behind some of the weirdest scientific phenomena on the planet.

Kids For A Clean Environment
www.kidsface.org/
Get the latest on environmental issues and learn how you can participate in cleaning up the planet.

Chemistry Books:

Why Chemistry Matters series. Crabtree Publishing, 2009. This series uses common examples from everyday life to help explain basic chemistry.

Science Fair Projects: Chemistry, by Bob Bonnet and Dan Keen. Sterling Publishing, 2000. Check out this book to learn how to do dozens of cool chemistry experiments at home.

Molecules, by Bonnie Juettner. KidHaven Press, 2005. This book provides information on atoms, molecules, changes of state, and extreme states of matter.

Matter, by Rebecca Hunter. Raintree, 2001. This book explains what happens to atoms and molecules in various states of matter.

Step into Science series. Crabtree Publishing, 2010. Each book in this series explores a step in the scientific method.

How to Reduce Your Carbon Footprint, by Amanda Bishop. Crabtree Publishing, 2008. This book teaches you more about the science behind climate change, the dangers of fossil fuels, and tips for conserving energy in your home and community.

Places to Learn More:

Chemical Heritage Foundation
Philadelphia, Pennsylvania
The Chemical Heritage Foundation is an organization devoted to sharing the history of and importance of chemistry through exhibits, events, and education. Check out its website at: www.chemheritage.org

American Museum of Science and Energy
Oak Ridge, Tennessee
This museum was designed to teach visitors about energy, especially nuclear energy. This is a great place to learn more about chemical reactions and the energy of matter.

Glossary

asthma A respiratory condition that makes it difficult to breath and is often caused by allergies

coal tar A thick black chemical liquid produced when coal is distilled

consistent Having a regular style or pattern

contaminants Something that contaminates or makes impure

distillation The process of heating a substance to produce a vapor, which is then cooled and condensed, in order to purify, concentrate, or extract parts from a substance

emissions Something discharged into the environment

equations A statement in arithmetic that uses an equal sign to show the equality of two quantities (3 + 3 = 6 is an equation.)

nobleman A man of high rank or title

particles A tiny amount

pesticides Chemical substances used to kill insects that harm plants and crops

physicist A scientist who studies the science that deals with matter and energy, their qualities, and the relationships between them

residues A substance or quantity that remains after a part has been removed or after a process has been completed

revolutionized Radically altered or transformed

simulates To imitate or reproduce the appearance, sound, or other external characteristics

substances Matter with uniform properties

synthetic Something made from chemical synthesis, especially something that imitates a natural product

theories Ideas not yet proven

Index